THE BELWIN STRING BUILDER

By Samuel Applebaum

FOREWORD

The Belwin String Builder is a string class Method in which the Violin, Viola, Cello and Bass play together throughout. Each book, however, is a complete unit and may be used separately for class or individual instruction.

In the opening of Volume III the pupil is taught to find the fingers in the third position on all strings. Simple shifts are introduced, followed by shifts to and from the third position with different fingers. Each type of shift is presented and developed with interesting melodies. The pupil is taught how to build major and minor scales and to play them with the basic bowings, the détaché, martelé, wrist and finger stroke, and the spiccato.

The material in this volume is chosen for its musical interest and its technical value. There are a number of duets which are to be played by either two pupils or with the class divided into two groups. There also are a number of melodies in which the class becomes a string ensemble, each instrument playing a different part. A small "p" after the number indicates there is a piano part for that melody.

The material in this book is realistically graded so that only a minimum of explanatory material is required.

TECHNICAL PROGRESSION

The Third Position (3rd P.)

Slide the entire hand up the fingerboard (from the elbow joint) until the 1st finger reaches the 3rd finger. As in the 1st position, the thumb is placed opposite the 1st finger or a bit behind it, with a space between the base of the thumb and the neck.

Finding the Fingers on the G and D Strings

On the G and D strings, there is a half-step between the 3rd and 4th fingers.

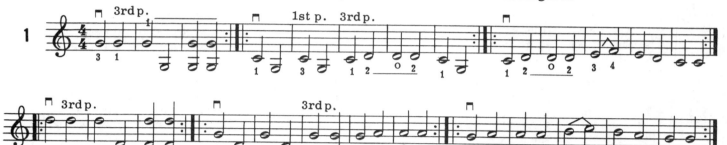

The Détaché Above the Middle of the Bow (A.M.)

Play smoothly from the middle to as near the tip as possible. Use the full width of the hair, drawing the bow parallel to the bridge. Only the forearm is to be used.

"t" means to test the note with the open string. Leave the finger on the string while testing.

We Take Off! (Duet)

F. WOHLFAHRT

ROTE PROJECT: In the 3rd position - practice the 3 4 finger pattern on the G and D strings. There will be a half-step between the 3rd and 4th fingers. Play in various rhythms and bowings.

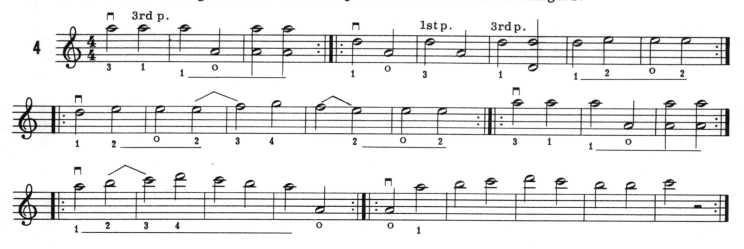 ...

Finding the Fingers on the A and E Strings

On the A and E strings there is a half-step between the 2nd and 3rd fingers.

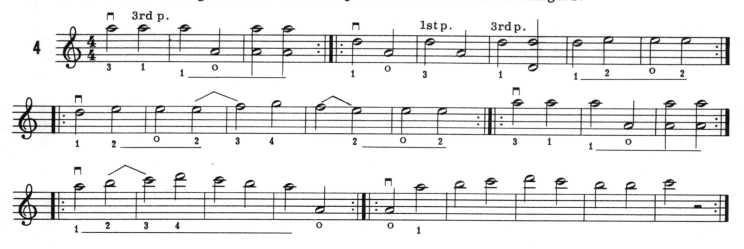

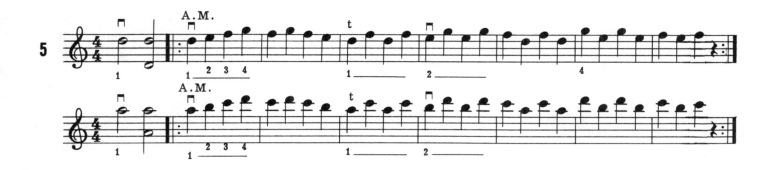

Jeanie With The Light Brown Hair

Moderato (Key of G)

STEPHEN FOSTER

ROTE PROJECT: In the 3rd position - practice the 2 3 finger pattern on the A and E strings. There will be a half-step between the 2nd and 3rd fingers. Play in various rhythms and bowings.

4

From One String to Another in the Third Position

The Détaché Below the Middle of the Bow (B.M.)

Playing from the frog to the middle of the bow, use the upper arm, which moves downward and a bit backward. The side of the hair is used with the stick tilted slightly towards the scroll.

Etude

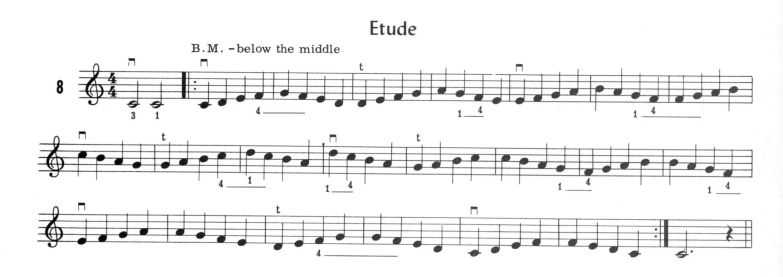

Home On The Range

The small note is to be stopped by the finger but not sounded.

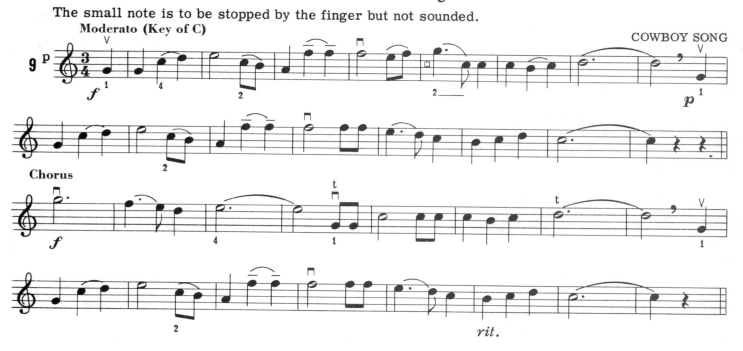

ROTE PROJECT: The C Major Scale in two octaves in the 3rd position. Play each note 4, 3, and 2 times, and finally each note once. Practice in various speeds and bowings.

More Melodies From One String to Another

Etude

Onward Christian Soldiers

ARTHUR SULLIVAN

Chorus

In The Sweet By And By

TRADITIONAL

NOTE . . . The class may now start the "Orchestral Bowing Etudes" for String Orchestra - an Etude for each bowing by Samuel Applebaum. This Etude Book teaches all the orchestral bowings and is played in unison with piano accompaniment. It is indispensable for the string section of an orchestra.

E.L. 1556

Melodies in C Major that Include the Third Position

mezzo-forte (*mf*) means that you are to play moderately loud.

Landler

GERMAN DANCE

Pledge To The Flag

EARLY AMERICAN MELODY

The Sun Is On The Land And Sea (Ensemble)

FREDERICK C. MAKER

NOTE . . . . To develop good intonation with the various styles of bowing we may now start SCALES FOR STRINGS - Volumes I and II by Samuel Applebaum. In this book the scales are presented in various rhythms and bowings. To help develop a stronger feeling of tonality, pieces and rounds are included in each key.

We Go From an Open String to the Second Finger in the Third Position

Sailing Above The Clouds

C. HOHMANN

Fairy Reel

IRISH DANCE

Noah's Ark

COLLEGE SONG

ROTE PROJECT: Learning to play in the high positions with the fast bow. Play the first finger pattern six times, then repeat an octave higher. Use a fast whole bow for each separate quarter note. Divide the bow evenly for the others. Refer to the Addenda of the Teacher's Manual for additional directions. (Rote Projects - Basic exercise No. 3)

6 times each

E. L. 1556

Melodies that Shift To and From the Third Position with the Same Finger

The shift upward is made with the entire hand, the thumb moving with the finger and not lagging behind. On the downward shift, the thumb moves in advance of the finger. During the slide you must lighten the finger pressure on the string and relax the thumb pressure on the neck.

We Shift with the First Finger

In Old Virginia

Allegretto (Key of G)

EARLY AMERICAN TUNE

Chorus

We Shift with the Second Finger

Ellen Bayne

Andantino (Key of C)

STEPHEN FOSTER

NOTE . . . The pupil will now be prepared to play the following: FOR STRING ORCHESTRA - 1. To A Wild Rose, E. MacDowell; 2. Gypsy Dance, H. Lichner. SOLO - Hungarian Suite by B. Bartok. This solo should be used for school demonstrations or for recitals. If possible it should be memorized.

More Melodies that Shift with the Same Finger
We Shift with the Third Finger

Travelling (Duet)

F. WOHLFAHRT

Moderato (Key of F)

We Shift with the Fourth Finger

Ups And Downs

Moderato (Key of C)

T. HENNING

NOTE . . . For pleasure and for the development of musicianship, nothing will surpass playing duets. In DUETS FOR STRINGS, Volume III, by Samuel Applebaum, the pupil will find many lovely duets to play with classmates or with members of their family. These duets may be played with another Violin, Viola, Cello or Bass.

E. L. 1556

The Scale Line Shift

When we shift to a note that is a step above, we slide upward with the finger that we are going to. When we shift to a note that is a step below, we shift downward with the finger that is on the string. In the following shifting exercises, the small notes are not to be played. They merely serve as a guide to the finger that is sliding. The pitch of the small note is approximate.

Gentleness

Moderato (Key of D)   NETHERLAND FOLK SONG

Only With Thine Eyes (Ensemble)

Melody Moderato (Key of D)   LOWELL MASON

ROTE PROJECT: To develop fluent shifting, practice No. 28 in different rhythms.
For example:

Melodies that Shift To and From the Third Position with Different Fingers

The 1st finger slides up until it reaches the 3rd position or the approximate pitch of the small note. The 2nd finger then drops on the string. On the downward shift, the finger that is on the string slides down until it reaches the 1st position. When we shift to a different finger, the slide is performed with the finger that is on the string.

The 1st Finger Shifts to the 2nd Finger in the 3rd Position

The Cowboy Goes Courtin'

COWBOY SONG

The 1st Finger Shifts to the 3rd Finger in the 3rd Position

Our Bright Summer Days Are Gone

STEPHEN FOSTER

ROTE PROJECT: The vibrato may now be started. Play the note A in the third position with the second finger on the D string. The finger must be well squared, using only the tip of the finger. Move the left thumb slightly behind the first finger. See that the knuckle of the first finger leaves the neck. There should be no contact between the left side of the first finger and the neck of the Violin. Roll the finger tip in eighth notes, first on the note and then slightly below in the direction of the string. The movement should come from the hand in the wrist joint. The Addenda to the Teacher's Manual will supply the remaining directions.

More Melodies that Shift with Different Fingers
The 1st Finger Shifts to the 4th Finger in the 3rd Position

35

For Gretchen

Moderato (Key of G)

GERMAN FOLK SONG

36

The 2nd Finger Shifts to the 3rd Finger in the 3rd Position

37

The 2nd Finger Shifts to the 4th Finger in the 3rd Position

38

Dear Katherine

Allegretto (Key of F)

GERMAN FOLK SONG

39

ROTE PROJECT: Developing tone color and control of the bow. Practice the B♭ Major Scale in two ways as follows:

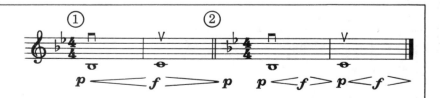

How to Shift When There is No Slur

When we shift and change bows at the same time, we slide upward with the finger that we are going to. We slide downward with the finger that is on the string. Do not permit the slide to be heard.

Oh, Susanna!

STEPHEN FOSTER

O What Fun!

GERMAN FOLK DANCE SONG

ROTE PROJECT: The Chromatic Scale to develop intonation. To be played two and four to a bow. Practice with both sets of fingerings. The bottom set is the conventional fingering and the top is the more modern set of fingering. With the top set of fingering, make sure that the thumb remains stationary and does not move with the finger change.

How to Build a Minor Scale

Here is a C Major Scale. Let us play it. **43**

If we start from the 6th note of this Major scale and build another scale, we have a minor scale.

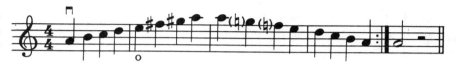

If we raise the 6th and 7th steps of this minor scale and lower them on the way down, we have a melodic minor scale. This is the form of the minor scale we will use at present.

This minor scale is called A minor because it starts on A. It is "related" to the C Major scale and we call it the "relative" minor of C Major because we started on the 6th step of the C Major scale. It also has the same signature as C Major.

An Evening Song (Duet)

C. HOHMANN

NOTE . . . The pupil is now ready to play the following: FOR STRING ORCHESTRA - 1. Theme and Variations, G. Papini 2. Ninette At Court, L. Saint Amans. SOLO - Elves' Dance (Perpetual Motion), C. Bohm. This solo should be used for school demonstrations or for recitals. If possible, it should be memorized.

Melodies in Minor Keys
Menuett (Duet)

Building a Melodic Minor Scale on E

Here is a G Major scale. Let us play it. **46**

If we start from the 6th note of this scale and build another scale, we have a minor scale.

If we raise the 6th and 7th steps of this minor scale and lower them on the way down, we have a melodic minor scale.

This minor scale is called E minor because it starts on E. It is the relative minor of G Major because it has the same signature.

Some Sadness

ROTE PROJECT: The Collé Bowing. This stroke starts with the bow on the string. Place the bow firmly on the string about two inches from the frog with all the fingers curved. Press the bow firmly into the string by pinching the bow. Release the pressure. At the instant that this pressure is released, the bow leaves the string, with the fingers straightening out in a spring-like action in the direction of the down-bow. When playing the collé up-bow, start with the fingers straight, and as the bow leaves the string in the direction of the up-bow, the fingers become curved. The bow travels above the string about two inches. Play any scale in slow quarter notes, repeating each note four times. Practice in two ways:
    1. All down-bows (from curved fingers to straight).   2. All up-bows (from straight fingers to curved).

E. L. 1556

More Melodies in Minor Keys

Building a Melodic Minor Scale on D

The D minor scale is related to the F Major scale because it has the same signature (one flat).
Notice that the 6th and 7th steps are raised on the way up and lowered on the way down.

The Hope

Moderato (Key of D minor)

HEBREW MELODY

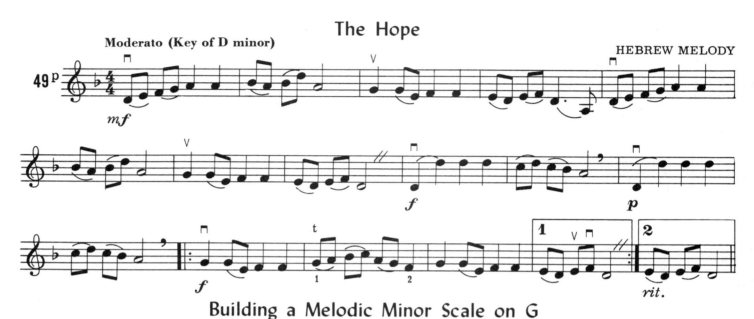

Building a Melodic Minor Scale on G

The G minor scale is related to the Bb Major scale because it has the same signature (two flats).

A Lively Dance

Allegretto (Key of G minor)

FRENCH FOLK SONG

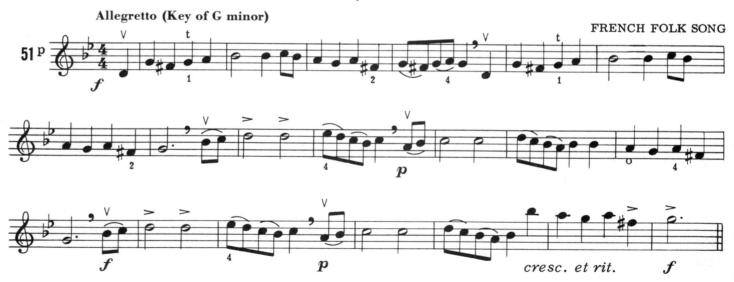

ROTE PROJECT: Play from memory one-octave melodic minor scales in the keys of A, E, D and G minor. Practice in various bowings and rhythms.

E.L. 1556

The Wrist and Finger Stroke

Place the bow on the D string about four inches from the frog with all the fingers curved. Make sure that the little finger is well curved, and that the middle joint of the thumb is bent outward. Draw the bow down with the wrist about two inches straightening the fingers at the same time. Now draw the bow up about two inches curving the fingers. Practice this stroke a few minutes each day. Use the wrist and finger stroke for the 8th notes on this page. Practice them in two places: about four inches from the frog and about one inch below the middle of the bow.

The Wrist and Finger Faddle

In A Hurry

Space Travel

ROTE PROJECT: Developing a fast bow stroke. Play one-octave Major and minor Scales in the following ways: Play the slow bow stroke (♩.) near the bridge, and the fast bow stroke (♩) near the fingerboard.

FAST UP-BOW

FAST DOWN-BOW

E.L.1556

18

Sixteenth Notes

Four sixteenth notes receive one count.

Use the détaché bowing above the middle of the bow.

On Roller Skates

An Eighth and Two Sixteenth Notes Receive One Count

ROTE PROJECT: The Grand Martelé - the whole bow martelé. This bowing should be practiced daily for many years. Starting at the frog, with fingers curved, press the bow into the string. Release the grip and draw the bow simultaneously. When you arrive at the tip, grip the bow firmly again, with the full width of the hair. The attack on the up-bow must be as strong as the attack on the down-bow. At the frog, this attack is made by a pinching of the bow with an upward pressure of the thumb. At the tip, the attack is created by a slight rotary motion of the forearm, which is the turning inward of the lower arm at the elbow joint. Practice in quarter notes ten times on each string, or with a scale, playing each note twice.

The Dotted Eighth and Sixteenth Note

A dotted 8th and 16th together will receive one count.

Fairy Belle

STEPHEN FOSTER

Awake, My Soul (Ensemble)

GEORGE F. HANDEL

The pupil is now advanced enough to play the two following selections: 1. Hungarian Airs, B. Bartok - 2. Serenade For Strings, W.A. Mozart. For additional information on how to teach the Spiccato, Staccato, Sautille and Riccochet bowings, refer to "Building Technic With Beautiful Music", Volume IV, by Samuel Applebaum.

More Melodies with Dotted Eighth and Sixteenth Notes

Leave a clean stop between the dotted eighth and sixteenth note when they are to be played in one bow and marked with dots.

A Merry Shout

Love's Old Sweet Song

ROTE PROJECT: The Spiccato Bowing. Play scales Major and minor, using the spiccato bowing. Repeat each note four times and then two times. Practice in two ways: 1. About three inches from the frog, using the hand only. The bow is actually thrown on the string from a height of about an inch, with a small swinging of the hand in the wrist joint. The fingers must be very flexible. 2. At the middle of the bow. In this form of spiccato, the bow is thrown on the string but the action stems from the elbow. The lower arm is used, with a flexible hand and fingers.

Melodies Using the Martelé Bowing

Practice in three ways: (1) Whole Bow (W.B.) (2) Upper Half (U½) (3) Lower Half (L½)

Sweet Betsy From Pike

Moderato (Key of D)

AMERICAN TRADITIONAL

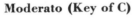

We Combine the Martelé Below and Above the Middle of the Bow

Early To Rise (Duet)

Moderato (Key of C)

F. MAZAS

ROTE PROJECT: Play a one-octave scale on the G string, using only the first finger, starting from the open string. When the first finger reaches the fourth note of the scale (third position) the base of the palm must lightly touch the rib of the Violin. When the first finger reaches the sixth note of the scale (note E - fifth position) the left thumb is to be at right angles to the neck in contact with the neck, midway between the middle joint and the tip. For the 7th and 8th notes of the scale, the thumb is not to move, ascending or descending. Be sure that the thumb moves with the finger when playing the 2nd, 3rd and 4th notes in the scale. Practice two, then four to a bow, on all strings. Practice the same scale, left hand pizzicato (without the bow).

22

Melodies with Double Stops

Aim for beautiful tone quality. When playing double-stops, incline the bow slightly towards the lower string.

Cadet Rousselle

FRENCH FOLK SONG

For My Son, Wolfgang (Duet)

LEOPOLD MOZART

ROTE PROJECT: A new style of bowing. Play one-octave Major and minor Scales in the following manner: Practice near the frog using the spiccato bowing.

E. L. 1556

More Melodies with Double Stops
Melody on Two Strings

Prelude (Duet)

F. WOHLFAHRT

Chords on Three Strings

Play the two lower notes at the frog near the fingerboard using about two inches of bow. Go immediately to the two upper notes playing them near the bridge. Hold the two upper notes for two full counts.

ROTE PROJECT: Developing the relationship between the first and fourth fingers with harmonics. Practice the following portion of the Major Scale on all strings in whole notes, half notes and quarter notes.

A New Rhythm - Triplets

When three 8th notes are grouped together and marked with an italic "3", they are called triplets. The three together receive one count.

73

My Peppy Pup Peter

Allegretto (Key of A minor)

HELLER

74

Action!

Allegro (Key of C)

H. SITT

75

The Martelé Stroke with Chords on Three Strings

Press the bow firmly into the middle string of the chord about two inches from the frog. Release this pressure and draw the bow quickly at the same time using the lower half of the bow. Try to play the three strings simultaneously.

76

NOTE . . . The String Orchestra is now advanced enough to play the two following selections: 1. Minuet For Strings (from Concerto Grosso No. 5) by G.F. Handel 2. Sonatina For Strings, M. Clementi.

We Build a Major Scale on the Note A

Notice the sharps before C, F and G. We raise these notes so that there will be a half-step between the 3rd and 4th notes, and the 7th and 8th notes. When we build a Major scale on A, every F, C, and G will be sharped.

The A Major Scale

If we place the three sharps in the signature it will mean that every F, C, and G throughout the piece will be raised.

The Roller Coaster (Duet)

F. WOHLFAHRT

Moderato (Key of A)

ROTE PROJECT: Developing a well-poised bow arm. Draw the whole bow about one inch above the string. Make sure that the bow remains parallel to the bridge at all times. Try to keep the bow from either touching the string or from rising more than one inch above the string. Practice in whole notes, half notes and quarter notes.

Melodies in Various Rhythms
Once To Every Man And Nation

WELSH HYMN MELODY

Norwegian National Hymn (Ensemble)

R. NORDRAAK

ROTE PROJECT: The one-minute stroke. Developing bow control. Draw the bow on the string as slowly and softly as possible. The object is to draw one bow stroke for sixty seconds. There will be a tendency to hold your breath during the bow stroke. Avoid this by taking a slight breath during the stroke. Practice on the open strings.

We Build a Major Scale on the Note E Flat

Notice the flats E, A and B. We lower these notes so that there will be a half-step between the 3rd and 4th notes and the 7th and 8th notes. When we build a Major scale on E flat, every B, E, and A will be flatted.

The E Flat Major Scale

If we place the three flats in the signature it will mean that every B, E and A throughout the piece will be lowered.

Cornish May Song

ENGLISH FOLK SONG

Isle Of Beauty

THOMAS H. BAYLY

ROTE PROJECT: The half-minute stroke to develop bow control and a beautiful tone. Draw the bow on two open strings for thirty seconds. The object is to play softly and to continue the sound of both strings throughout the stroke.

How to Play Harmonics

One full step above the 4th finger in the 3rd position on each string, we will find a harmonic which is an octave higher than the open string. The hand remains in the 3rd position while the 4th finger flattens out and stretches to the harmonic. A clear harmonic will be produced if the string is lightly touched in the right spot. The other fingers are to be lifted from the string.

I Have Bon Bons

Allegretto (Key of G)

FRENCH FOLK SONG

ROTE PROJECT: The Staccato Bowing. Try to play as many notes as possible above the middle of the bow. Practice in the following rhythms:

Beautiful Melodies with Harmonics

In the 7th measure the hand remains in the 3rd position while the 1st finger reaches back for the F#.

There Was A Shepherd

Allegretto (Key of G)

FRENCH FOLK SONG

Loch Lomond

Andante (Key of F)

SCOTCH FOLK SONG

Chorus

Butterflies

Allegretto (Key of B♭)

J. STREABBOG

Fine

D. C. al Fine

NOTE . . . The pupils will now be prepared to play the following: FOR STRING ORCHESTRA - 1. Sarabande, Carl Bohm 2. Air Varie, Opus 89, No. 5, Charles Dancla SOLO - Two Guitars, Russian Gypsy Folk Song, by Samuel Applebaum. This solo may be used for school demonstrations or for recitals.

Melodies that Will Prepare for the Spiccato Stroke

The following melodies are to be played about four inches from the frog using only the wrist and fingers. There is to be a slight pause between each note. Use very little bow - no more than about two inches.

On The Stairs

Melody (Ensemble)

The Dancing Elves

ROTE PROJECT: Developing the Sautille bowing. This is played around the middle of the bow. Play the first finger on the D string (note E) with the wrist and finger stroke, using about one and one-half inches of bow. Start with slow 8th notes, gradually getting faster and faster until the bow rebounds from the string by its own momentum. Hold the bow loosely with the first three fingers. The little finger may leave the bow. Do this for about three or four seconds at a time, then stop and start again, in order to avoid any tension of the right arm. Do this a few minutes daily for many months.

How To Play the Spiccato Stroke

The spiccato stroke is similiar to the preparatory stroke on Page 30. Now however, we will lift the bow from the string during the stop instead of allowing it to remain on the string. The bow is actually thrown on the string from a height of about an inch with a small swinging of the hand in the wrist joint. The fingers must be very flexible. Use the side of the hair and strike the string a bit nearer to the fingerboard than to the bridge. Play these pieces about four inches from the frog.

Ping Pong

F. WOHLFAHRT

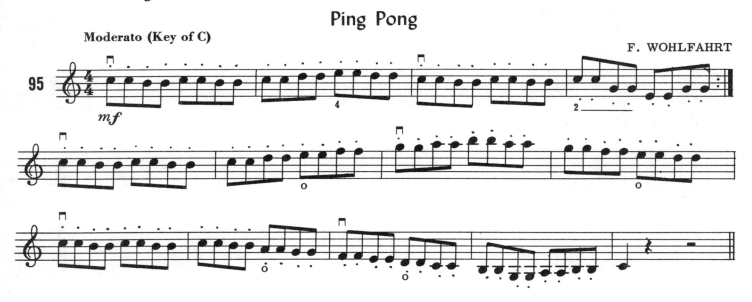

A Merry Dance

The spiccato stroke is not to be used for the quarter notes. They are to be played broadly.

SLOVAK FOLK SONG

Perpetual Motion

R. HOFMANN

ROTE PROJECT: The Arpeggio stroke. Play a series of three and four string arpeggios about the middle of the bow. Do this gradually faster and faster until the bow rebounds from the string on each note by its own momentum.

Lively Melodies Using the Spiccato Stroke

Use the spiccato stroke on all the 8th notes marked with dots, and a smooth détaché stroke on the quarter notes. You must manage to have the bow about four inches from the frog when you are to again start the spiccato stroke.

ROTE PROJECT: Developing the Riccochét bowing. Drop the bow on the string about an inch or two above the middle, from a height of about an inch above the string. After the drop, relax the grip on the bow, allowing it to re-bound. Use no more than two inches for the down-bow, and practically no bow at all for the up-bow. Pinch the bow slightly to stop the re-bound. Practice in the following rhythms: